Developing the Heart of a Leader

The Beginning of the History of Leondar

Ashton Fourie

Other Books by Ashton

Real Dreams

When you lose yourself ... do you know where to go looking
for you?

The Three Primary Resources

Table of Contents

The true revolutionary is guided by strong feelings of love.

Every day we must struggle so that this love is transformed

into concrete acts that will serve as an example

- Che Guevara, before he left his position of official leadership in Cuba to continue his fight for socialism in other parts of the world.

People have asked me why God allows poverty, famine, war

oppression of the weak and the victory of the wicked over

innocent people.

I have always refrained from asking this question, for I am

afraid that God would ask this same question, of me.

- Unknown Author

Foreword

In 2003, at the age of 33, I had the privilege of having a year of holiday in China. During this time I dedicated my time to prayer, reading about leadership, and writing this book. I was also studying towards a bachelor's degree in management at the time. After my holiday, I kind of forgot about the book, until around 2008 when I remembered it, dug it up from the archives, and was quite surprised to find that after a further five years of experience and on-going leadership studies, I not only still agreed with everything I had written, but actually recognized that if I had remembered some of it, I would have been able to avoid some of the mistakes I'd made as a leader.

But still I did not publish it.

Some more time passed, and in 2015 I remembered again that I still had this manuscript that was very close to ready. By this time, however, I had in the meanwhile obtained a master's degree in managing and leading innovation and change. Surely by now with all that new knowledge, and five more years of exposure to international management in both small and larger organisations would have changed my ideas about leadership. But to my surprise, as I was proofreading it again, I found myself only making a few small changes here and there – simply because my writing skills have improved a bit, not because my fundamental philosophies on leadership has changed.

And so I am now finally publishing this book. The one thing I have come to realize in the 12 years since I'd written it, is that some of the things written here are much easier written than done. But I firmly believe that if you want to become a great leader, you will have to start deep within and develop your leader heart.

Ashton
22 May 2015
Xiamen, China

Prologue

"My fellow villagers!" Shorban's loud, clear voice commanded veneration even through the cold hatred in the air. "The time has come for me to lay down my leadership in this village and for Rennan, my son, to take my place."

"We don't need another oppressor!" The words rang through the morning air. There was an uncomfortable shuffle in the crowd.

Without reply, but with clear deliberation, Shorban stepped down from the platform as Rennan ascended. A low murmur rolled through the crowd like the ominous rumbling of far-away thunder. The person who had shouted the objection was a friend of Rennan's from childhood. Everybody knew that. Shorban's eyes were resting on Rennan, cold, expectant.

Rennan made a small nod to someone close to where the voice had come from. There was a cry of pain followed by a shocked silence as people opened a space around the dead young man. The guard returned to the front of the assembly, wiping his sword unceremoniously.

Rennan immediately tightened the grip with which his father had ruled the village. With an iron fist he trained his first band of soldiers personally.

Village after village was taken. He carefully selected the weakest villages to be conquered first. His modus operandi was simple and effective. He executed the leaders, appointed his own leaders and took for his campaign the best young men. Soon he had taken over leadership of all the surrounding villages, and began making plans for building a kingdom. Carefully he selected the natural leaders and trained them in the principles of leadership, both in war and in government. He taught his best riders to draw maps, using symbols to represent all the information he required. Within a year, Rennan had a well-trained, well-equipped force of just more than five hundred men and a set of maps covering the whole area he intended to conquer.

For five bloody years the campaign continued, until finally, the last and largest of all the villages fell. Rennan called his country Leondar. It stretched from the Land of the Merchants to the mighty Lands of the Kings.

His well-trained army and his fame in war ensured Leondar's peace, both internally and along its well-guarded borders. At the least sign of treason, heads would roll. Thus made King Rennan his government and it was ostensibly untouchable.

And so, many years passed.

Under Rennan's leadership, Leondar had become more prosperous than the wealthy Land of the Merchants and more powerful than any of the Lands of the Kings. The people, however, remained desperately poor, suffering under the hard yoke of taxes the local governors laid upon them. But as Rennan grew older, instead of becoming increasingly secure in his power, fear began to grip his heart as he saw a slow increase in the amount of uprisings he had to keep suppressing.

There came a day when he knew that the end had become inevitable.

The arrow hit him between his shoulders.

He felt his bodyguard closing around him, heard the voices, heard the sounds of many arrows being shot, and the clashing of steel against steel.

King Rennan saw his whole kingdom flash before his eyes — hundreds of thousands of poor people, living with the bare necessities, day after day working from sunrise to sunset to pay their taxes; hundreds of executions; angry mobs...

And then all went black.

The Division of Leondar

PURPOSE:

Knowing and fulfilling your own purpose, and teaching others to know and fulfil theirs, this is the core of leadership

Once upon a time in the Great Land of Leondar, the Great King Suran, ruler over all Leondar, was talking to one of his advisors who had just travelled through the kingdom to collect the taxes.

"I see that every year Selsan's half of the kingdom brings in a much larger amount of tax than Nashin's," The king remarked.

"Yes, your majesty," answered Cresan, his chief advisor, "Nashin says it is because of the great difficulties they face in the North, as opposed to the easy conditions of the people in the South."

Suran was concerned that Nashin was becoming increasingly unhappy with the portion of the kingdom he had received—so much so that he was beginning to fear possible mutiny from that side.

Some days later he called for a secret meeting with Cresan, his oldest wisest and most trusted councillor, and his Chief Messenger, a young man whom he had been watching for some time and had begun to respect for his desire to learn, his keen insight into matters of government and his distinct concern for the welfare of the people.

*   *   *

It was a fine summer's day when the horsemen rode into the Castle of North Leondar. The front rider, clad in the uniform of a High Advisor of the King of All Leondar, was as well known throughout the land as was the Great King Suran himself.

Nashin, ruler of North Leondar hurried towards them bowing low. Knowing Nashin's dismal record as a ruler, the shallow attempts at winning favour by paying excessive respects did nothing other than irritate Cresan.

During lunch, Cresan inquired into the condition of the land.

Nashin's response was a continuous complaining about the difficult conditions in the mountain regions, his lazy people, and the dangers of the wild animals in the mountains and so on and so forth.

After they had finished their meal, Cresan addressed Nashin and his leaders:

"I have come to bring you and your people some good news:

The division of the land is about to change. The new border between the two halves of the country will run from North to South. You will be the ruler in the West and Selsan will be the ruler in the East.

The Big River will be the dividing line in the Southern plains. In the Northern Mountains, the Dragon's Back will be the border."

The "Dragon's Back" was a ridge of mountains forming a watershed between the East and the West of the Northern Mountains.

"And when will this take effect?" Nashin asked, hardly able to conceal his greedy excitement. The Southern Plains were famous for their fertility and had brought the ruler of South Leondar great wealth.

"Another messenger should reach Selsan about this same time, and as soon as we receive the signal, a line of giant torches will be lit along the new border. These are already being erected as we speak."

*   *   *

The Castle of South Leondar rose against the red sunset sky, as the Royal Chief Messenger rode into the Southern Gate City, where the Big River emptied into the ocean. Two riders from the southern Ruler's personal guard met him and escorted him to the Great Castle.

He requested to see Selsan, ruler of South Leondar, as soon as possible and was shown without delay to a spacious room. A writing desk by the window overlooked the bustling harbour. One wall was covered with maps representing different aspects of Selsan's territory: agricultural developments, communications, roads and major rivers, merchant routes, and defence infrastructure. The rest of the walls were filled floor to ceiling with shelves of books and scrolls.

Whilst waiting for the famous Selsan to arrive, the Chief Messenger's eye fell on a piece of framed scroll. The handwriting was like that of a child learning to write:

"Having seen the wealth of my king, and the poverty of my father, I resolve today to become the man I will need to be, to change the destinies of the poor people of Leondar.

Signed on this 24th day of the Thirteenth year of the Rule of King Rennan

Selsan, Son of Gerodor, Peasant of Leondar"

The Messenger thought back of what Cresan had told him about Selsan, the night before he had left for the great castle of the South.

"When he was still a boy he had learnt from anyone who was willing to teach him, to read and write. As he grew up, he was always asking questions. I watched him become a man of integrity. I watched him walk with unwavering principles in a society where it was accepted that survival depended on how well you could lie and cheat. And later I found out that every night, he studied and thought and wrote.

"He was about thirteen when he first started trying to encourage people to dream - just small simple things - encouraging them to want to become better people and helping them find ways to achieve these dreams. It

5

seemed insignificant in a society where all were treated as slaves. Most people laughed at him. Rennan never paid him any attention. But more and more people began to listen when he spoke."

The Messenger took out a little note book he always carried with him and wrote:

~~~

The process of becoming a leader:
- *Determine the kind of person you want to be*
- *Plot for yourself a course, to become that person*
- *Whilst walking this road, learn to help and inspire others, to become the people that they want to be*

~~~

His thoughts were interrupted by Selsan entering the room.

Selsan enquired after the welfare of his king. In his countenance and manner the Messenger saw real interest.

The Messenger in turn asked Selsan after his own welfare. Talking about the affairs of his region, Selsan became animated with passion. He was most thrilled about the fact that according to his recorders, there was now not one family in the South of Leondar without at least one person doing work enough to afford for the family a safe and dry place to stay, education for the youngsters, and healthy meals every day.

The Messenger made another note in his little book:

~~~

Leaders have passion for the welfare of their people

~~~

He really wanted to know how this remarkable feat had been achieved.

"It had to start in my own heart." Selsan explained, "When I first took over the region, I really wasn't sure what the job of a Regional Governor was.

~~~

To lead others with purpose, first discover your own purpose

~~~

"So I had to take much time thinking about my purpose as a person, and then my purpose as a leader. Only then did I begin to be able to understand the purpose of those leaders I had to lead. People need purpose, and leadership must help them find their purpose.

~~~

The purpose of leadership is to improve the lives of the people you are leading

~~~

"Once I understood our purpose as the leadership of these people, I knew we had the responsibility of helping these people to feed, house, clothe and educate themselves. I thought that, because the region is good for agriculture, people could all farm.

"My plan was simple enough, and seemed certain to succeed. I thought that farming was not difficult – something anyone can do. I distributed the land so every family had a small piece of ground to farm and make a living. However, this project failed. For some, it was great, but some people seemed to degenerate into even deeper poverty than before."

"Why?" The Messenger was quite surprised at this. He had read about the first project in South Leondar and how the quality of life for so many people improved so quickly.

"At first," Selsan continued, "I thought some people were just lazy and didn't want to work. But then I thought to myself that someone would have to be really, really lazy, to not want to work so much that he would see his children not having food to eat. I began to change my heart, and I reminded myself to believe in my people.

~~~

Change starts in the heart of the leader
First, believe in your people and then seek to understand them

~~~

"So I went back to travelling and I spoke to the poor people. I found few of them lazy. I learnt that most people have a deep desire to work hard and succeed. I found some who were very discouraged.

~~~

To understand the problems, you have to understand the people

~~~

I found that over time, the initial set-up of fair distribution of land changed, because some people simply excelled at farming, and soon became rich from it, whilst others failed dismally, and soon became poorer and poorer – almost like slaves to the rich farmers. Farming is not difficult, but if there are people around who really excel at the business of farming, then even an average farmer will soon find it difficult to make a living in the face of the stringent competition.

~~~

Pursuing activities in line with one's natural talents and interests greatly enhances one's chances of success

~~~

"I began to realize that some people cannot farm. Some detest farming. Every day to them, is a burden. For the "natural" farmers, every day is a joy. So I thought to myself that for someone who hated farming and had no talent for farming, life must have become increasingly difficult with every passing day. The "naturals" excelled, and the competition was unfair.

~~~

Continually working outside of your natural design, will first erode your ability to enjoy your tasks, and then systematically erode your ability to be successful and to contribute meaningfully to your society

~~~

"I didn't want to take anything away from the farmers. Destroying that which was succeeding hardly seemed like a wise way to try and repair that which was failing.

"However, I noticed with the farmland now being utilized as well as it was, there was a great surplus of food in every region. Some of this was eaten by the poor people – but there was still left over. I realized that successful farming had created a new resource which needed to be utilized – excess farm produce.

~~~

Match people's natural talents and interests to available resources, and train them to apply those in the best way

~~~

"That is when I began to speak to the Land of the Merchants. Some of the people who couldn't farm, could surely trade. In fact, when talking to some people, I discovered that some of them loved to trade. In order to ensure that their natural talents would be best applied, I paid some merchants from the Land of the Merchants to come and teach and work with groups of people I had identified. Our own traders became highly skilled, and by the time this project was completed, they were able to help other potential youngsters to enter into trading.

"Soon more and more of my region's activities began to depend on trade. In a region like this, I needed to begin to know how much money was moving around. So I needed to begin to employ money recorders, who would keep track of the money in my region.

~~~

The two primary roles of leadership:
- *Developing people*
- *Creating an environment conducive to maximum performance*

~~~

"People began to realize that the boats they were using were not big enough and were unable to traverse the seas, so they started paying some people to start building boats. Then the roads were too small, and much time was wasted in the rainy season, because some roads became too muddy to travel with ease. People began to learn that they could build really good roads with small river-pebbles. We started levying a toll on the use of roads for commercial purposes, and used the proceeds to create road-building teams. They purchased the pebbles from farmers who had pieces of river on their farms. All these activities improved trade, and trade ensured that money became more and more available to pay for these activities.

"By developing the resource of farm land as well as we could, we started a chain reaction which turned things we had never even thought of, into resources. All that remained to do was to help the governors of the towns to begin to understand the interests and the skills of their people, match the people to the needs and the resources, and begin to train the people in accordance with these developments.

~~~

Prosperity follows the accurate matching of people to resources

~~~

"The more I developed the people, the more efficiently they could use the resources, and with every new resource I began to utilize in my region, a wealth of opportunities around the control and application of those resources sprung up, so that today, almost every person in my region can perform a duty they can enjoy and be proud of."

"So you simply match the people to the resources and challenges." The Messenger summarized, thinking how simple and easy this approach now sounded.

"But, forgive me for not sharing your total confidence in mankind – surely there must have been some people, in this surge of prosperity, who had learnt that they could get by without having to work, maybe by begging or using their children to beg – as we notice everywhere else in the kingdom and as we hear from our messengers, is even still not absent in the wealthy Land of the Merchants. Do you want to tell me that every person found something he or she wanted to do?"

~~~

The leader must care not only for the successful, but also for those who are failing

~~~

"No," admitted Selsan. "You are right. Even once we had created opportunities enough for everyone, there were still some who chose not to utilize these opportunities. At first I was tempted to simply outlaw begging and living on the streets, but then I remembered that we have to always first believe the best of the people – so for those who were failing, we needed to create an opportunity to recover. We first created a small hostel in every village, which was run and initially funded by the local government.

"At these hostels, people were provided with food, clothing and clean accommodation. To earn their living, they did manual labour throughout the village, sometimes for the village government and sometimes for private people.

"If people didn't want to improve themselves, they remained labourers, and they stayed under supervision indefinitely. Those who wanted to improve themselves could learn new skills, paid for by the local government, including skills needed to identify opportunities of involvement in the economic community.

"By creating a place which could effectively absorb the homeless, I felt that it was now reasonable to outlaw the beggars and homeless from the streets and have them taken to these shelters. I've just had a report. Not one case of someone being found begging or sleeping in the streets has been recorded for more than a week."

*To create a culture of productivity, laziness must meet with penalty and
hard work must meet with incentive and opportunity*

"I must congratulate you." The Messenger truly felt that this was undeniably one of the most significant achievements he had ever heard of.

"But I'm sure you didn't come to just hear of our success! There must be a message from King Suran for me?" Selsan enquired.

Having caught on to the fact that Selsan mentioned the building of boats, and having seen the large number of wooden structures in the city, the Messenger had concluded that Selsan's region must utilize vast quantities of wood. He carefully prodded in this direction and found that Selsan was indeed in desperate need of timber. Nashin's inefficiency had caused timber to be expensive and scarce, to the point that Selsan had started purchasing wood from the Land of the Kings. Knowing that the northern mountains were mostly covered with dense forests, the Messenger carefully broke the idea of the changing of the land's borders. It was received with great enthusiasm.

A week later, the giant torches began to flare, creating a fiery line between the two newly defined regions.

Almost as soon as the torches started burning, a migration started in the Southern plains of people moving from the West, which would now be Nashin's land, to the East – the parts that would remain under Selsan's rule. Although Selsan felt somewhat flattered by this clear practical display of support for him, he also realized that the best skilled and most talented people would migrate, because they had the confidence to be successful everywhere, leaving the poor and unskilled people of the land to fend for themselves. Furthermore he was deeply concerned that the eastern planes could not support such a sudden increase in population, and that cities would begin to suffer from the many evils that come with overcrowding.

He called for an emergency meeting of all the governors of the South west in the public square of one of the largest central villages. He hadn't been to this village for a few years, and he was very impressed when he saw the condition of the village. The streets were all paved, and there were strips of grass alongside every road. Every house was whitewashed with lime, and they had torches lighting the roadside by night. He realized that if all these people migrated, a lot of this would fall into disrepair, and he feared that Nashin's leadership would never be able to recreate this environment of prosperity.

Teach your leaders the higher purpose of serving those below them

Selsan spoke for a long time, calling upon all he had taught them over the years. He assured them of his confidence of their being able to lead even under the most adverse conditions, and that they didn't need him. He reminded them of their responsibilities, not only to those in their land who had been successful, but also to the poor who could not afford to relocate.

He reminded them that their purpose as leaders was not simply to lead successful regions, but that they had a responsibility to every person in their regions, to make sure they were looked after.

He tried to unite their hearts in a shared purpose to continue being successful, even when they were under a leadership they could not trust. The test of their true leadership ability lay before them.

In conclusion, he pledged to them his support and assistance as far as was within his ability. Whether they chose to stay or relocate, he would support their decision, and he would do everything to try and help them be successful.

Selsan wanted to also call on them to ask their people to stay, but he decided against that. He realized that this was every leader's own decision. He was the leader of the governors. He could only lay this request at their feet. He could not impose on them what they had to do with their people. Each of them had to decide for himself how he would respond. Each had to communicate to his people in his own way.

Nashin's Campaign of Self Destruction

DEPTH OF CHARACTER:
**It's the HEART of the leader
that wins the loyalty of the HEARTS of the people**

When Nashin heard that Selsan had called a meeting of the rulers of his new villages, he immediately assumed that Selsan was trying to convince his people to move to the East, so he could hold on to the hard-working intelligent people he had. The Northern people were lazy and not very clever.

Nashin immediately set off for the Great Palace of Leondar. It was about two day's ride from the Castle of the North. The last glows of the setting sun could still be seen on the tips of only the highest towers as Nashin and his entourage rode into castle. His demand for an immediate audience with the king was granted.

After the normal bowing and paying respects required upon entering the throne room, Nashin began his rage.

He expressed his intense dissatisfaction at the fact that Selsan would be allowed to campaign in what was no longer his territory. He expressed his concern about losing the skill, the intelligence and the diligence of the Southern People. He complained that it would take many years to relocate the Northern people to the planes, and that their laziness and lack of intelligence would make it near impossible to redevelop the country to the condition where it was today.

~~~

Always seek first to understand a situation, before making assumptions

~~~

Before Nashin could finish, the Great King Suran interrupted him angrily:

"Nashin, have you made any inquiry into the nature of Selsan's campaign in the West?"

Nashin had to admit that he had made no inquiry – but circumstances were clear and time would only be wasted through such inquiry.

"In fact," retorted King Suran, "very little time needed be wasted. You could have, when walking into my palace, requested first to have an audience with the person whom I have appointed as Recorder and Councillor of the affairs of this transition in Selsan's region. I advise you speak to him, that you may gain greater insight into the matter."

King Suran without any further word, got up, and walked out of the throne room, his face glowing with anger and frustration both at Nashin's arrogance and incompetence but even more frustrated at himself for having allowed Nashin to remain ruler of that region for so long. He knew Nashin had support amongst some powerful people in his court, and he was always afraid of revolt, should he remove Nashin from office.

Whilst Nashin was still thinking upon what the king had just told him, a young man dressed as a mere messenger appeared from the Council chambers and invited Nashin to join him. Having never taken note of anyone that didn't seem to have the rank of at least councillor; Nashin didn't recognize that this was the Royal Chief Messenger.

~~~

Fear of people will destroy your ability to execute the right decisions

~~~

"The King says you would have some questions regarding Selsan's campaign," the young messenger started, "I am well informed and can probably give you the answers."

Somewhat annoyed at being sent a lowly messenger, Nashin decided nevertheless to oblige, as he did not want to offend the King's hospitality. People have died for lesser offences.

"Well, my first question is whether you know if the king is intending to take any action to stop Selsan from campaigning." Started Nashin, wondering who this person was, but unwilling to ask, because the calm and confident manner with which he addressed Nashin, was unusual in lowly servants.

"On this, I can assure you the king will take no action."

"So the king is just going to allow Selsan to drain from the good land all the good people?" Nashin's face was red with anger and frustration, as he spat out these words.

"I think you are making some assumptions that are not based on a good understanding of Selsan's principles." The Messenger disliked Nashin intensely. He was always surprised that someone with such shallow insight into even the most elementary matters could have survived for so long as a leader and he felt no inclination to be of any assistance other than what was specifically asked of him.

"Well, I see there remains nothing for me to do, but to go down to the South myself, and try to counter this campaign."

As Nashin was leaving, the Messenger looked after him with an expression of pity mixed with contempt. If Nashin had been more patient, and had spent more time understanding, he would have rather focused his efforts on the North, where even his own people were secretly slipping through the mountain passes to Selsan's new side of the land.

Although it had been declared illegal in the Northern Mountains to migrate, there existed no accurate record of the people and where they lived. It was impossible to guard the myriads of small passes connecting the East and the West. Even along the well-guarded main routes, some of Nashin's own guard had begun to move their possessions to the East.

It was about ten days later, when Nashin, with a guard of two hundred armed men, entered the south western plane of Leondar.

As they were traveling, Nashin saw wagons with people traveling at just about every intersection. To his surprise they were returning to the land, not leaving.

To him this simply didn't make sense. Why were the people seemingly all revolting against Selsan's campaign? Had he totally overestimated Selsan's ability? Maybe the people had heard that Nashin had gone to the king, and were afraid the king would relocate them by force.

The meeting at the first village was swiftly arranged.

~~~

A weak character will typically develop a set of tools and skills that enables the leader to exert power and influence over other people through techniques such as intimidation and manipulation

~~~

"Dear Men and Women of West Leondar, I greet you!" Nashin began.

"I have seen how you have all begun to return, despite Selsan's efforts to win you all over to his side." There was a murmur amongst the people. Nashin thought the people clearly were still upset. Possibly Selsan had done something to make himself generally disliked.

"However, I assure you that you will be looked after and protected in the west of Leondar. I plan to speak to Selsan myself. There will be no more interference from him on this side of our borders." This was again met with a murmur, and one of the councillors of the village seemed to beckon to him that he wanted to speak to him. However, Nashin felt he had the people's attention, and wanted to make the best use of this opportunity.

"If required, we will protect you by force, from any interference from the East. I have brought with me only a small portion of my powerful

15

army and I will readily dispatch as many soldiers as is needed to protect you." At this the murmur changed to a general commotion. The councillors were beginning to be surrounded by little groups of people obviously asking them all sorts of questions. Nashin couldn't understand what was causing this commotion. The people now seemed more concerned than ever.

One of the councillors succeeded in escaping the crowd and jumped on to the platform next to Nashin.

"I think you have misunderstood something," he began, "the people are returning because Selsan has asked the governors to return. There is little reason to expect that Selsan would interfere with something he endorsed. Selsan was afraid the land would fall into disrepair, and the good work that had been done, would be lost."

Nashin looked at the councillor incredulously. He turned to his chief advisor.

"Why had I not been told this before?" he growled, under his breath. "Now I have made a fool of myself in front of this village, and the news will spread. I will not be made a fool of!"

The Advisor turned pale. With a movement of Nashin's hand, the execution of his chief advisor was commanded, and within seconds, completed.

After another moment, Nashin decided that he had made his point, and he commanded his horse to be brought. Within a few minutes, Nashin and his guard had left the village.

The news of this occurrence spread very quickly. Nashin continued to travel the South, trying to inspire confidence, but when he began his return to the North, he noticed with rage more wagons than what he had seen returning, now crossing the Big River to the East.

He could understand that the people would be upset because he had been misinformed, but he had shown his commitment to rectifying problems by dealing with that error in the most severe way. He could not understand why they seemed to reject his leadership still.

~~~

Judging reasonable mistakes in an unreasonable way, will not promote confidence in leadership

~~~

He was enraged at all his advisers, for having given him bad advice. The great King Suran's Messenger had withheld critical information from him – and he started believing that this might have been King Suran's whole plan. From the beginning King Suran had always seemed to favour Selsan above him. He always seemed to do things to help Selsan and to undermine Nashin.

When he returned to his palace and started receiving the updated reports, he realized that while he had been undoing the good Selsan had done for him in the South, his own people had been deserting him in the North.

Nashin immediately called together his personal guard and commanded them to guard the routes across the mountains, personally. Anybody who wanted to desert western Leondar was to be executed immediately. They were to have no mercy. It was critical that people learnt quickly that this behaviour would not be tolerated.

His scheme worked to an extent. The migration of people in the North slowly decreased and eventually stopped. Nashin had no way of determining the true damage, because he hadn't known previously how many people had lived in his region.

Nashin also sent messengers into the East, telling people that anybody from the Northern regions will be given land on the Southern Planes.

He implemented this plan very swiftly and appointed one of his governors to oversee the allocation of land in the South. This scheme had some success, and some people returned to the West, to receive their land in the South.

~~~

Intimidation and access to good resources can sometimes seem to produce results despite bad leadership

~~~

Selsan Deals with Change

VISION
- will help you know where you want to lead your people to

PLANNING
- will help you know how to lead your people there

COMMUNICATION
 - will help your people to understand your vision and your Plan

EXECUTION ABILITY
- will help your people get to where they agreed to go with you

CHARACTER
- will make your people trust in you and stay with you when:
... the dark clouds blur the VISION
... the winds of change drive the ship off the course of the PLAN
... the thunder and rain drowns your COMMUNICATION
... the waves breaking over the ship prevent all EXECUTION

Selsan's castle, normally a reasonably quiet place, was a hive of activity. Recorders were arriving from all over the new territory, continuously updating the population records and maps. Selsan had followed Nashin's "campaign" with interest, and he realized that after what Nashin had done, he could not blame his people for moving.

However, this presented him with a thorny challenge. The burden on the land had just about been doubled. Migrants had settled wherever they had been able to find a place, and many of them were lacking the bare necessities for survival. Winter was only four months away. A crime wave swept through the country as these people tried to survive, and some farmers lost more than half their crops to theft.

The sudden increased traffic of heavily laden wagons caused the roads to deteriorate quickly and some of the overloaded wagons would break down in the roads, causing obstructions which in turn hindered the flow of goods to the river harbours – hindering trade.

Selsan responded by immediately calling for emergency meetings throughout the southern regions. He drew up a message which was to be read publicly to hundreds of gatherings of both migrants and local residents. He called upon the migrants to refrain from stealing, and upon the residents to give what they could. He was trying to prevent the migrants from having to steal just to survive. From his side he committed that his government would immediately begin to do everything in their ability to ensure that the crisis would be dealt with swiftly and efficiently.

His armed forces were all immediately called up to assist the existing police and the punishment for theft was made considerably more severe.

He also dispatched some of his army to patrol the roads, assist with repairs of broken wagons, and to continually return reports of places where roads needed mending.

Selsan realized that international trading would initially have to be controlled, because he would need the food in the country to feed the extra people. He was also afraid that some people would begin to exploit the helpless state of the migrants. He feared that they would charge exorbitant prices for food, or even force these people to trade the few possessions which they had brought with them, for food.

~~~

Leadership must protect those against whom odds have become
unreasonably stacked by uncontrollable changes

~~~

He had a meeting with his councillors and governors to devise a plan to deal with the financial burden of caring for the migrants until they could become self-sustaining again. A temporary export tax was implemented. The tax was not high enough to discourage all exports, but it created a new source of income which was to be distributed to the migrants to help them to purchase food within Leondar. They also imposed a freeze on all prices of goods essential for survival, so that exploitation could not take place.

Heralds were once again immediately dispatched to pronounce these two arrangements. Selsan's representatives in every town were responsible for ensuring that the price freeze was adhered to and people were made aware of where they could go to should they wish to report any exploitation or breaking of the new laws. He established a special office at the sea harbour and the land border posts for collecting the special export tax.

~~~

The structure to uphold a decision is as important as the making of the
decision

~~~

After a few weeks, the reports about the change in the migration in the North began to reach him. Many people in the North were moving across to Nashin's territory, from where they were relocated to the Southwest.

Selsan immediately saw an opportunity to repopulate his new northern territories, and so relieve some of the burden from his southern territory.

For the next three days, he met with five of his best leaders. As always, he began the meetings by making sure the people whom he wanted to be in charge of this project, understood his heart and what the core purpose of the project was. He then reduced his involvement to advice and asking pertinent questions while these five men took responsibility and ownership of the project.

~~~

Delegation starts with communicating the heart of the leader

~~~

He regularly reminded them of the importance of the people, reminded them that this was the purpose of the project – to create opportunities for people so that every person can work and earn a living.

They worked fast. They dispatched recorders at high speed to the North to go and record the current status and return with the information as soon as they could.

Within three days the outline of the project was ready, and within a week the recorders were able to supply the information needed.

~~~

You can plan with vague information, but to finalize decisions, every effort must be made to have the most accurate information available

~~~

Approximately 10% of the population would be willing to migrate. Selsan knew this number would be higher once he started communicating the project. There were currently enough deserted houses in the North to accommodate about 2% of this number.

He immediately began taking from the plan the ideas he felt would appeal to the people. With this as a starting point, he sketched a short and long term plan, tried to think of all the troubles and problems they would face, and prepared contingency plans for these.

Using all of this, he built his message. He thought about every word and every sentence. The success of the project depended largely on the people's response to his words. If the people accepted it, it could work. If they didn't it would fail.

People's hearts are moved by words.
Choosing the right words is as essential as creating the right plans

After two weeks Selsan left the humming activity of the castle and began a tour of all the major villages.

His address was the same in every village:

"Dear People of East Leondar!

"As you know, the migrants from the West had good land and good property. They are hard-working people like you, who have been successful. However, they have, by the recent actions of Nashin, been convinced that they could not stay under his rule. I am sure many of you would have felt the same, had you been in their shoes.

~~~

The best resources, the best plans, the best ideas,
... will all come to nothing, if you fail to rally the hearts of the people

~~~

"I therefore ask you to treat these people with respect and dignity, just as you would have wanted to be treated were the positions reversed.

"In the course of history, things sometimes happen, outside of the control of the people that are influenced, which suddenly shift the odds against one group of people in a significant way. It is then up to the leadership of those people, to create some rules that will protect them from being totally destroyed. It is up to us to continually ensure that the field on which you are all playing this game of life, is kept reasonably fair.

"The export tax law and the law of the freeze on prices are both temporary laws. As soon as the migrants have been absorbed in our society, these laws will be abolished. It is in everybody's best interests that you help and assist these people to become part of your communities and to find places for themselves in your local societies and economies as soon as possible.

~~~

Create real incentives for meeting objectives

~~~

"As soon as a village is reported to have absorbed all the migrants in its area of responsibility by having involved every one of them in some part of its economy, the temporary laws on that village will be lifted. Goods from that village will be marked by my local recorder, and those goods will be allowed to be traded again without the export taxes at a value determined by the free market."

At this point Selsan stopped, and answered the questions of the villagers. Once they all seemed satisfied, he continued to reveal the plan for the North.

"Now as many of you know, some time ago we started planting some forests towards the North, but these were taking up precious farmland, and it would be many years before these trees would reach an age where they could be used.

"Well, this brings us to the logic behind the change Great King Suran has implemented. The resources of Leondar are now better distributed between the two regions, and we now have a very large territory of natural forests which we can begin to utilize.

~~~
*A good leader shows the opportunity in every change*
~~~

"For this project, we will need many different kinds of people.

"The first people we need are builders, town engineers and woodcutters. There are already many villages, but they are badly designed and there are not enough houses. We need a leader for every village, and we need teams that will build houses, fix the existing houses, clear larger areas around the houses and so forth. We need to prepare the villages for new inhabitants.

~~~
*Selsan started not with the need for the infrastructure, but with the need for the people to create the infrastructure*
~~~

"The next groups of people we will need will be more builders and engineers who have worked on the construction of bridges and large buildings. This part of the project will be the building of an infrastructure of roads and waterways.

~~~
*People create the environment*
*To change the environment, use the people*
~~~

22

"The areas we clear around the villages will provide wood for the building of houses in those villages. The wood we clear for the roads, will be transported to the south, where, as you all know, we are in continual need of wood.

"We will also need some of our farmers to go up and learn about forestry, to ensure we plant trees at the same rate at which we cut them down, and to help monitor the growth rate of these trees – so we don't run out of wood in the future."

Selsan then answered questions again, and immediately after this, his recorder recorded the names of those interested in moving to the North, as well as their skills and the work they would want to do.

In the meantime, in the big city, the blacksmiths were working day and night, under commission of the leaders of this project, to make tools that would be needed for taming the northern forests. They were determined that by the time the first people would move to the North, they would be well equipped with everything they could possibly need.

~~~

If you want to be successful, make sure you give your people the tools to do the job

~~~

It took about four weeks for Selsan to complete his communications campaign. He had appointed some of his messengers to dress as villagers move among the people, and ask questions, so that he could understand the people's sentiments and morale. From their feedback he was confident his people were positive and full of hope for the future.

In the palace, several storerooms had been filled with the equipment needed, and the whole courtyard was full of new wagons. Selsan decided that whilst morale was high, and his message was still in the hearts of the people, they had to start moving.

For two days the road from the western gate looked like a small river of cattle, as the oxen steadily poured into the city, hooked up their wagons, and were then led along the Northern Road out of the city, towards the North.

Messengers on horseback were being sent ahead, to ensure all who had volunteered to go to the North and had been selected for this first migration were ready by the time the wagons reached them.

The King's Chief Messenger, who was now also recorder for Selsan's region, made a point of staying as close to Selsan as his duties would allow throughout this project. He tried to learn by watching Selsan work, and he tried to understand why Selsan did the things he did.

The success with which Selsan had rallied the hearts of the people into this project for the North amazed the Messenger. Everybody knew that the North had been known as just about uninhabitable. Wild beasts, thick forests, severe climate changes, a complete lack of level ground – all of these made the North a place where few people in their right minds would voluntarily venture into.

He would have thought that many people would have lost confidence in Selsan, after he failed to keep the western people in the western part of the country, but after his first communications campaign they rather seemed to all rally together and soon the crime wave also subsided.

Apart from the recording he had been doing for his normal duties, he had continued to keep a journal in which he wrote down what he had learnt, and whenever he was traveling, he would pore over these writings, think about them, and in the evenings he would add his own thoughts.

One evening, after returning from a journey specifically focused on recording the results of Selsan's campaign for the project to the North, he sat poring over all he had recorded. He then began to write a summary of what he believed to be the reason for Selsan's success, in this project, and finally, he concluded with this:

"All of these can really be summarized into Selsan having developed a very great ability to inspire AND maintain people's confidence and motivation, and this he uses to create and drive his vision.

"This is all about communication, planning, execution, but underlying all of this, seems to be simply the people's belief in who Selsan is as a person and a leader, and I think that is in turn somehow fuelled by Selsan's belief in the fundamental goodness and capability of his people."

~~~

Successful leadership rests on the ability to inspire and maintain people's confidence and motivation, and to create and drive a vision.
Inspiration comes from communication
Creating and driving a vision, is a skill of planning and execution

~~~

As soon as the first wagons started leaving the city, Selsan called for the recorders and representatives from the South, to prepare for a meeting. He gave himself one day to rest and recover after his travels. He wanted to be sure he was in his best spirits for addressing the next part of his current challenges.

Selsan started his meeting by thanking everyone for the hard work they had been doing. Although he hadn't seen any of the reports, he knew these people, and he had been able to see, walking around the castle, how everyone was head down, working without pause. He didn't need to see any reports to know they had been doing their best.

Selsan wasn't concerned for the existing residents, or the existing government structures. He had learnt early in his career as a leader to put fences around change and crisis. He had learnt that, whilst a tremendous effort might be needed to deal with certain problems, some people have to continue doing the normal day-to-day work. For this reason, as soon as the migration had started, he appointed some people, outside of the normal existing structures, to begin working on the problems related to the migration. This placed a lot of extra burden on his own court, since he had to provide some of his best leaders to oversee this process, but he knew having them there, looking forward and setting direction whilst everyone else were dealing with crisis, was the surest way to get back to calmer waters.

~~~

When the boat is leaking, it might seem most important to scoop water – but it is better to also have someone fix the leak and someone row you to the shore, rather than having everyone absorbed by the need to scoop the water

~~~

He first called on the most junior recorder in the room to speak.

The man reported that he was well taken care of by the cities where he travelled, and that he seldom needed to use his allowance, because the cities provided in his every need.

However, what pleased Selsan the most was that the migrants were now being treated in the same way. In all the villages surrounding Dedlom, where this man was recording, there were no more migrants living in temporary shacks or in their wagons next to the roads. They had all been accommodated. Some of them, admittedly, in small rooms that previously served as stables and sheds, but even these had been cleaned and washed, so that they were now quite comfortable and dry. In most of the towns, only a small portion of the governmental funds were being used to care for these people, and most of the merchants and farmers were selling to the migrants at prices much lower than to the local people.

These people were, however, battling to get integrated into the local economies, since most of the needs in every village were already well met, and the villages were small. There were few opportunities for the number of new entrants.

Selsan questioned two more junior recorders from other regions, and the answers, though differing in details, contained the same spirit. People

25

were being positive and helpful and the migrants were making an effort to become part of the communities.

He hoped that the Northern Migration would at least open some opportunities, as some of the current villagers would leave openings in the current local economic structures. He also knew that a large portion of the people who had wanted to go to the North, were from the migrants, so their numbers would also somewhat decrease, but he feared that all of this would not happen quickly enough.

There were still many migrants that had not found lodging, even though the local people were making efforts to make anything available. In the winter, all the animals had to be back in the sheds – so the migrants couldn't stay there through the winter. This process had to be accelerated.

In general, Selsan was very encouraged, as he requested his four district governors to take the podium.

Each of these governors had taken full responsibility and ownership for the problem. Not once did he hear a word of blame laid against the king, for having brought about this change, neither a hint of reproach against himself, for not having tried to talk the king out of this device of his.

"— And so we realized," the governor of the South western district which had received the most migrants, was saying, "— that the key to the solution of our problem, would be to increase the efficiency with which we are using our resources. Everybody was already working towards the same goals and purposes, but abundance had made us somewhat negligent in the management of our resources. Even though much food is being traded, enough was still wasted that, even whilst feeding all the migrants at no profit, we hardly saw a difference in the total income to our region.

"We did some more enquiries into this phenomenon and eventually found that what had happened is that the traders had always bought food from the farmers at a certain price, and sorted it afterwards. The best quality went for export, the second best sold locally, and the rest was thrown away. What used to be thrown away was not bad. It was just not the best – and this now became the food for the migrants – who were all very happy to receive food.

"The farmers then realized that, had they sorted the produce beforehand, they could have priced the good food higher and local food a bit lower, and could have focused on reducing production of the lowest quality food – focusing on increasing their quality, rather than just trying to produce more.

"One farming leader then made a daring suggestion, which took some time to digest, but we decided to implement it. I'd like to take a moment to repeat his story almost verbatim:

"'I have a little stream that runs through my farm,' he had begun, in the normal roundabout way of these farmers, 'and when I first got there, it was really just a strip of mud, about twenty meters wide, overgrown with reeds. When it rained, it would flow visibly, but the rest of the time, it would just be mud. I used to just ignore this piece, and pump water from my neighbour. But then my son decided he wanted to start 'his own' farm, so he asked me for that piece of ground. Of course I gave it to him, and he began to dig a small trench all along the middle of it. Very quickly, the mud started drying out, and all the water drained into this ditch. Within a week, he had a strip of twenty meters wide, with water running through the middle of it. He dug a bigger hole at the end of it, and lined it with clay, so that he now had a dam. By focusing the water, my son made both ground and water available. He simply removed the waste by implementing some control over the flow of the water.'

"His point was that in the way they've farmed, they probably were all wasting, because they hadn't been forced to focus their attention to getting the most out of every inch of ground.

"Discussions around this went to and fro and finally it was decided this farming leader would first do an experiment in his region, with the migrants that were there.

"The farms in Southern Leondar are all square blocks of equal size. So it was decided that a strip of one tenth would be cut between every four farms – so that a new farm was formed, which would be 40% the size of the existing farms. These new small farms would then be given to migrants who used to be farmers in their regions.

"This leader had a meeting with his farmers, and it was agreed with them, that, should the experiment fail, they would receive their land back. It would be an arrangement only for one season.

"We then had a meeting with the migrants, and we listed all those people interested in land. It was agreed to select the fortunate ones, by drawing lots. We made it very clear that this was an experiment, and that the ground was effectively only lent to them, for the first season.

"Some of the pieces of land had produce almost ready for harvesting, and to our great surprise, the farmers agreed to cut the 10% regardless of what was on it. So the migrants even received some pieces of ground harvest-ready, and some almost harvest ready.

"It is not possible to truly judge the success yet, but from the first harvests since, the farmers have reported that just through paying more attention to their harvesting methods they were able to reduce a lot of the bad quality. They also suddenly began to notice places where their furrows didn't run to the end of their property – so that there were often long stretches of unused land between two farms, much wider than what was needed for the harvesting carts. Others began to notice that their furrows were very unevenly spread, and started noticing that there seems to be a certain minimum distance between furrows, before one would start seeing the difference in the quality of the crops. So they have already begun taking more care to cut every furrow as close to the previous one, as they believe to be the best. Some claim to have added more than the 10% which they had lost in giving away in ground, by just doing this.

~~~

Abundance often causes waste
Shortage often increases the efficiency of application of resources,
providing even more than what was produced in the times of abundance

~~~

"They've begun to realize that there will always be bad produce in between, and some of the farmers have begun to throw these on heaps to rot, so they can use it as fertilizer, the next season. Other farmers have begun to cart the dung from the cattle farms to their farms, to fertilize the ground, as they believe that this will yield better crops."

Selsan sat listening with admiration. In another region, money was made available from the export taxes with which the migrants could purchase some land, and farmers were encouraged to offer some land for sale. These farmers used this money to improve the conditions of their current farms to get back to normal production.

In another region, farmers agreed to sell their goods for cheaper, and began similar methods of increasing production, without increasing their costs.

Everywhere the principle was the same. The sudden increase in requirement has taught the people to become more focused in the use of their resources. In response to his first communications campaign, the people had simply risen up and made the effort to succeed, even before he had been able to initiate and lead any projects of this nature.

~~~

Encourage success to breed success through cooperation and mentorship

~~~

Selsan spent some more time learning what was happening everywhere and then moved the meeting into a direction of beginning to plan how the successes from the different regions, can be applied in all the regions.

He also heard that the governors, expecting the migrants to become a severe burden on governmental funds, had already also increased the efficiency of their people through focusing their efforts on the things that were really the government's responsibility, and beginning to give some of the tasks they used to perform to some of the migrants, who started performing these for small fees that they collected directly from the people.

~~~

Focusing on purpose is powerful in continually reducing wasted effort and resources

~~~

One example was the cleaning of the water canals. The governors had explained that there would be shortage, and asked all the people to start cleaning just the piece of the water canals in front of their homes and shops. One of the migrants immediately saw the opportunity and for a nominal fee to every individual, he's cleaning the canals and making a good profit for himself.

Seeing this, Selsan realized that the governmental overhead on the land would not need to be greatly increased, but that the increase in people would increase his tax income, and so he immediately made a commitment to a small tax cut across the land, if they could achieve certain targets, which they were to set for themselves over the next few days.

However, he made one of the rules that the improvement also had to be across the land. If one region improved much more than another, no-one would benefit. He knew that the cooperation between the regions would be critical to ensure a constant sharing of the knowledge that had helped them improve. Already, by sharing what they had learnt that morning, every region had three new strategies that could all be applied simultaneously, to address their problems.

~~~

Incentivised cooperation will accelerate the distribution of knowledge

~~~

Almost One Year after the Changes

The LEADER:
- wants to be successful, for the sake of the people
- will be successful, because of the labour of the people
- can only be successful, if he believes in the people

And HIS PEOPLE
- want to be successful
- will succeed or fail, because of leadership
- can only be successful if they can believe in their leader

Once all the tax was collected, Nashin set off to the Great Castle of Leondar. On his arrival, he was shown to the Royal Treasury, where he declared his income, greater than ever before, and paid the required taxes. He felt proud as he walked away. Success was his at last.

After having been shown to his room, and been given opportunity to refresh himself, he was summoned to the throne room.

The Great King Suran looked in high spirits.

"Well, Nashin, I see things have really turned for you!" the king called out as Nashin walked in.

"Yes, your majesty," replied Nashin as he bowed, "Indeed I am greatly indebted to you for the opportunity you have given me. You have always looked after my interests, and I must compliment you on the great wisdom with which you rule the wonderful land of Leondar."

With many more compliments and nice sounding words, Nashin gave his praises to the Great King Suran, who quickly found himself getting bored with this narration and annoyed by its shallowness.

"OK, let's get to business." The king interrupted him, getting up from his throne and walking to the Council Chambers.

Nashin obediently followed. In the Chambers, he found Cresan and that annoying Messenger that had deceived him the previous year.

"Now, Nashin, Cresan has recorded here, the tax that you submitted this year. It is indeed a much greater sum than last year. However, I would have expected you to bring in at least half of what the South brought in last year. Yet this number is somewhat smaller. Can you tell me what the hardships were that you had faced, and how you dealt with them?"

Nashin was somewhat taken aback. He didn't know how much Selsan had submitted the previous year. He now realized he never knew just how much the South was producing. He just always knew it was much more than the North. However, he was not going to be caught off guard. Words and quick thoughts were his strong point, and they had gotten him out of many a spot of bother.

"Well, Your Highness, as you know, most of Selsan's people chose to move to the East, despite both his and my attempts at trying to convince them to stay."

"Yes, I recall that I was given some information about a dismal failure of your campaign, in this regard. You have all my sympathy." The king commented, his voice betraying no sympathy of any kind.

"Thank you, Your Majesty. I turned this into an opportunity though, and moved a large part of the population from the North into the South. In fact, quite a large number of my people moved from the East, obviously also preferring the leadership they had been used to, and wanting to use this opportunity to make a better living.

"However, as you know, these people were now settling in an area where they had not lived before, and they had to learn the ways of the land. I am sure that over time, the production will increase, and soon match the former levels of production."

Nashin was certain that Selsan's people in the South, being all used to farming, would have made a pretty number – so many hands to work the ground can only bring in good revenue. He thought it would be wise to bring this under the king's attention.

"Selsan, on the other hand, is fortunate enough to have increased the number of people that were used to working the land, and I'm sure that this year his production will look considerably better. However, I think you will find that in the North, where the conditions are adverse, the production would have dropped, because the population migrated, and I don't think any people from the South would have wanted to move north."

"Have we received the final revenue figures from Selsan?" he asked of Cresan.

"Not yet, Your Majesty. Selsan was reported to be expected in about an hour, according to the gongs."

"But we have some information regarding the population movements in his country, don't we?" the King had now turned to the Messenger.

Nashin was astounded to learn that the population in the North east was now made up of more former southerners than northerners. Most of the Northern people, even those that had previously lived there, had moved south, and people from the South had moved north. He could hardly imagine these figures to be accurate.

They then continued to discuss some more general affairs regarding peace and stability. There had been some warring and fighting in Nashin's region – especially in the South. Nashin explained that this was just because people were disputing land ownership in the beginning. His efficient personal guard had sorted out everything and all was now peaceful.

A while later, a messenger delivered a note to Cresan and within a few minutes Selsan was announced.

When asked about the impact of the change, now a year later, Selsan began to expound on the difficulties the people had faced, and how his governors and the people had worked together, to overcome the difficulties. He praised his people for their willingness to take on the challenge of the North, and the innovation with which they had begun to develop ways of utilizing the small waterways, to get wood out of the mountains down to the Big River, from where it could be floated to different river harbours. He was expecting that they would be able to start exporting within the next two or three years, which would really bring a new boost of income for the mountain region.

He then praised the people in the South east, for the way in which they had absorbed the extra people. He expounded on the way in which they had learnt to focus their resources better, eliminating waste, and how this had solved most of their problems. He was most delighted that his people had succeeded in getting everyone into a warm dry place of accommodation before the start of the winter, without having had to compromise the shelters of the livestock.

~~~

Leadership is about letting your people achieve the results, and letting them take the glory for their success

~~~

When he thanked the Great King Suran for this decision, one could see that the gratitude was really from his heart. He couldn't help but comment on the great foresight of the king, for most of his governors, and he had to admit, even himself (though he had never let his people know) had at first thought that this change would not be for the good. However, it had brought out the best in his people, and had also now provided him with an ample supply of timber, which had previously been in short supply.

The Chief Messenger was, as was always the case when he had the opportunity of hearing Selsan speak, listening with keen interest. In his mind he was making a short list of what Selsan seemed to think were the keys to his success:

Keys to Selsan's Success:

- *True pride and belief in his people, and humility regarding his own influence*

- *A healthy leadership structure*

- *Vision*

- *The ability to plant little pieces of his big vision, in the hearts of his people*

- *Allowing people to get on with their work*

- *Matching people to resources, opportunities and problems*

- *Seeing every problem, opportunity and resource in terms of the kind of people needed to deal with it*

- *Learning from everyone*

- *Creating a learning environment throughout his region*

- *Encouraging and incentivizing cooperation*

- *Passion for the welfare of his people because he had ...*

  ☐ *Real concern for his people*

- *Continually refocusing his leaders to the purpose of their existence i.e. the people*

- *Continually refocusing the people and their efforts back to the purpose of a given task, project or organization*

- *A continuous process of receiving and giving pertinent communication*

Clearly the people were the most important key – Selsan could not mention enough, the good his people had done.

However, the Messenger knew that people needed leadership and organization to do a good job, so he also added a healthy leadership structure to his list.

Although Selsan never took praise for having had a great vision, he was continuously encouraging his people to see solutions to their problems. He turned his people into visionaries. Then he simply let them get on with their work. The Messenger couldn't but suspect that Selsan himself always had a burning vision of what he would like to see achieved in his region.

However, he also was continually reminding his people to keep focus of the purpose. The purpose of his leaders was to look after the people. Every project had a purpose, and the purpose was always people focused – Selsan made sure he kept focusing his leaders back to that purpose.

Selsan was always communicating – either receiving reports with pertinent information, or communicating the purpose and vision. Selsan seldom gave orders. He allowed people to understand their problems, and get on with the solutions.

Selsan was forever shifting people around. Whenever a new problem or a new resource became available, Selsan first focused on the people that could either benefit from the resource, or solve the problem. He would invariably then create some plan for moving the people to the opportunity, need, or problem. It seemed to him as if in Selsan's mind a need, an opportunity and a problem were all the same – they were all an opportunity to give to someone to prove himself.

Selsan was always learning. Most of the solutions in his country were not Selsan's own solutions. He learnt from the people around him, and applied what he learnt with wisdom and insight.

Selsan was always encouraging cooperation.

But the thing that stood out, above everything else, for the Messenger, was Selsan's passion. Selsan seemed to care more for his people than anything else, and from this passion for the people, was born a passion for every project that was initiated, because he seemed to always keep in his mind the single purpose of: "The People"

It seemed as if Selsan's unwavering belief in the best of his people caused them to somehow just always live up to his expectations. Their desire to not disappoint a leader for whom they had so much respect, was a much greater motivator than the fear of failure with which Nashin was continually trying to drive his people.

Nashin tries his hand at Leadership

To BE a LEADER
You must first
BECOME a LEADER
To BECOME a LEADER
You must:
Develop within you the heart of a leader
Then
Develop within you the mind of a leader
Then
You will find yourself thinking, talking and walking like a leader

Upon his return Nashin set to work with great vehemence. He had learnt much from listening to Selsan and was now determined to make his region as good, if not better, than Selsan's.

The first thing he had noticed was that Selsan had appointed governors over every village, and each of these governors was held responsible for the welfare of his town. This explained how he so successfully worked with so many people. He just dealt with his few leaders, who dealt with the governors, who dealt with the people. So Nashin chose five of his best men. His most trusted man, he placed second in command to himself. The other four, he assigned to four regions – just like the East.

They had a meeting to discuss how they would improve things. Nashin, in his fury and self-centred jealousy, had not always heard everything Selsan had said. He was now trying to remember how Selsan got the four regions to each perform so equally well – but, failing to remember, he decided the best way would be through competition.

He immediately set a competition between the four governors. The one with the highest production would get certain tax cuts.

He remembered that Selsan was always talking about "winning the hearts" of his leaders, and "planting the vision in their hearts", so he made them discuss the competition for a while, and he also explained to them that the vision is for the West to produce more than the East. He assured them the people had just all been lazy, and a change in their leadership style would make all the difference.

Words seldom failed Nashin, and with many more words, he had them all very excited and full of zeal for the future. With the regions distributed, the four governors made their preparations, and were soon off to their new regions.

In the regions, they immediately began to set competition between the villages. They, in turn, also offered some incentives for the best villages.

In the North, the two governors each secretly slipped over to Selsan's side, to go and see what had been done there. What they saw discouraged, rather than enthused them.

Every major stream had been dammed up in all the narrowest places. The dams weren't very big, but they created stretches of water, which were used to float the logs along. At every dam wall, a big hoist had been constructed, which was driven by water, pressured through a tunnel in the bottom of the dam wall. This hoist was used to pick up the logs on the one side, and throw them into the next dam – from where they floated to the next wall.

Next to the rivers, roads had been cleared for easy access to the dams. Everywhere they found new roads that had been built. Every village had a clearance close to the river, fenced with spiked stakes, where they were growing enough fresh produce for the village and where their livestock were kept. Against almost every mountain, "rolling" paths had been cleared, where the logs were being rolled down to the rivers.

In every place where trees had been harvested they could see rows and rows of seedlings.

Having seen this, they realized that this was more than what any one of them could achieve by himself, but they continued to avoid asking each other for help, because each one was hoping that somehow he would be able to be more successful than the other, and at least get the tax break to help reduce the financial burden on his region.

Nashin succeeded in continually motivating them with his good speeches. They immediately got everyone who could do any blacksmith work, to start making tools. They started working in the South, where they were closest to the waterways, and began to clear paths along which the logs could be dragged by oxen. They didn't have the skill to build the water transport system Selsan's engineers had built, but they felt that with hard work, they could compensate for that.

Soon the first logs started coming out of the forests and floating in the river. They delegated some people to float the logs down to the first trading station.

However, here they met with more difficulties. Competition was tough, and Selsan's merchants had been trading for years. Their negotiation skills were well polished, and time after time they succeeded in getting their wood sold before the westerners.

In the mountains things were getting worse and worse. A few heavy showers had washed away most of the roads, and the mountain streams proved incapable of providing any assistance in getting the wood down to the river.

They began to realize that the success Selsan had achieved in the North was not the success of one year – that one year was just the result of many years of consistently building and improving the skills of his people. The builders of those roads must have built many roads before, and seen many floods. The makers of the tools had been making tools for years, and funds had been made available to make vast quantities of those tools in a short time. The traders were well versed in trading, knowing where to find the markets for which goods, and how to negotiate the best deals. The engineers, who had built the dams, must have been building large structures for many years. They thought of the large bridges crossing the Big River in the South and of the canals that provided water to the most outlying areas from the Big Lake – also the work of Selsan's engineers. The Great Palace, the City at the mouth of the Big River, the ships with which he sailed the international waters – all these were the results of years of ongoing building of engineering expertise.

~~~

Sustainable success can only be built through an ongoing process of development

~~~

In the South things were not going much better for Nashin. The production was continually going backwards as the competition between the regions became competition between the villages, and even competition between farmers. A large amount of energy was spent over land disputes. Villages were accusing each other of all sorts of corruption and misrepresentations of true production. Trust in the leadership structure Nashin had instituted, was deteriorating. Nashin was losing trust in his men, and his men were losing trust in their governors. The governors had no confidence in the ability of their people to sustain production. At the same time, the people had no confidence in the leadership of their governors. The people saw their leaders as people who were simply extracting taxes and doing as little as possible, other than increasing the tension in the land with their continual reminders of how important it was to win.

Reports from the two regions were continually reaching the Great Castle of Leondar. The Chief Messenger took a keen interest in following the events in Nashin's region, and he made a habit of thinking about the problems Nashin was facing.

He had noticed that lately it really seemed as if Nashin was beginning to try to do the right things. He personally didn't like the competition idea, but he could see that it could work very well, if implemented correctly. Also, the problems facing them in the North could be solved with some perseverance and hard work, but somehow the people seemed to just lose confidence in anything Nashin proposed before really trying to make it work.

The messenger still regularly travelled to Selsan's region, to carry correspondence between Selsan and King Suran. He made every effort to spend as much time observing Selsan as he could.

One evening as they were sitting on the roof of Selsan's castle, watching the sun set over the harbour, the Messenger mentioned his observations of Nashin's efforts to Selsan.

"I have really seen a change in the reports. Nashin is really trying, but he's failing." The messenger commented after giving Selsan an overview of some of the things that had happened.

"Look at that harbour, and tell me what you see." Selsan responded.

The messenger looked for a while. The harbour consisted of two parts. On the one side was the river harbour, and on the other side the sea harbour. Between the two harbours was a wide low bridge, used to transfer goods from the riverboats to the large ships.

"I see two harbours, some boats, the buildings of some boat companies, and some people transferring goods from ships to riverboats and from riverboats to the ships."

"Now look at those ships, and at the riverboats. What are the differences?"

"Well, the ships are much larger. They also have more sails."

"Right. Now why are the ships larger?"

"Because there is more space on the sea; and maybe because the sea is rougher. A larger vessel is more likely to survive a storm. They also carry more goods to another large port – I've often seen riverboats from several small river towns all load their entire loads into one ship – so the ship would take a variety of goods to its destiny."

"People are like those boats and ships. Every person has a capacity to do something. Some are those small boats you see being used to transport stuff from one side to the other side of the harbour. Other people are like the riverboats. They have simple sails and some oars to help them, but if they were to face one storm in the open sea, they would be torn to shreds.

Our ability to achieve is limited to who we are
To achieve more, become a bigger person

"The size of your heart and mind – the core of who you are as a person – that represents the size of your ship. As you face difficulties, as you think about things and work on building the right habits and thinking the right thoughts, you are enlarging your ship. The larger the ship, the more rough water you can handle, the more goods you can move around, the more people you can accommodate.

"The skills you acquire are like the special rudders, the different kinds of sails that are used in different winds, the well trained sea-men. The variety and quality of these skills also impact the kind of waters you can handle, the kind of storms you will be able to weather, the quickness with which you will be able to manoeuvre the ship.

Our character determines the size of our ship.
The skills that we have acquired are like the technology of the ship and the skill of its crew.
Together, these will determine the size of the opportunities and problems that we can negotiate

"Ships are built once – and that's the way they stay. All that can be changed is the skill of their crew.

"People however, determine in the course of their lives what the size of their hearts, and the skills of their minds are going to be, through the actions they perform continually. The great people you meet are simply normal people who had, through years of regular application, made themselves great.

"Nashin had never applied himself, and now he is suddenly faced with opportunity which he believes he never had before. He is trying to grab the opportunity, but because he has not grown as a person, and he had never applied himself to the process of acquiring the skills, he is not equal to the opportunity before him.

"Life will present opportunities. Whether you will be able to grab hold of those, will depend on what you had been doing, to prepare yourself, up to that point.

"It's like a fighter. Many people think it's the winning in the ring that makes a fighter a champion, but it's not. It's the years of training many hours every day that makes him a champion. The ring just provides an opportunity to prove that he is really the champion.

~~~

Life will present you, sooner or later, in the arena.
Whether you come out a champion, will depend not so much on what you
do at that time, but much more on what you have done up to that time.

~~~

"I want to tell you a story. You've probably heard the first part.

"There was once a young man who was very successful in the military. Before he quite knew it, he had received his commission as a general. He wrote to his father, and expressed his feelings of inadequacy. His father replied simply:

'Think like a general, walk like a general, talk like a general, and then you will be a general.'

"The young man applied this advice, but he found his life hard and strenuous. He eventually died from a heart attack at an early age. Do you know why?"

The Messenger thought for a while. He tried to put himself into that person's shoes. He tried to imagine himself suddenly having to command thousands of people, risking their lives in every decision, and he could see why it would be strenuous. What made the true generals that are old and wise, so different, so confident and calm whilst so many lives depended on their decisions?

"Because he only became a general on the outside?" he ventured, knowing that Selsan was always hammering on the importance of first developing your heart and then your mind, before developing the world around you.

"Exactly!" Selsan smiled broadly with satisfaction, and continued:

"Talk like a general, act like a general, walk like a general, and then you will be a general.

"In these simple words lie the hidden emptiness of much of the achievements of society, and herein lies the difference between the truly great, and those who look back with regret upon broken relationships, lost health and many other sacrifices, when their careers are over.

~~~

If our achievements are out of balance with who we essentially are, the
pressure of the demands of position will eventually cause us to burn out

~~~

"I am busy trying to make you a leader. This will take many years, and now we are only laying the foundations, but I want you to know, that in every one of these conversations, I am busy trying to help you to change yourself, from being a messenger, to being a leader. You have the potential, and I want to help you develop that potential.

~~~

The key to training a leader is not so much teaching him to know and do the right things, as to teach him to be the right man

~~~

"However, only you can become that leader. It's what you do consistently, every day when neither me, nor anyone else is watching, that will prove your leadership one day, suddenly, when the whole world is watching."

Selsan let the Messenger ponder awhile.

"So," the Messenger ventured after a while, "what you are saying is this:

'Become a general, then you will walk like a general, think like a general and talk like a general – and it will come naturally, without continuous strain and effort.'"

Selsan congratulated the young Messenger on his insight before expounding further:

"For any person, working is like a fire. Who you are, is like the coals for the fire, and success is like the blower that makes the fire burn hotter and hotter. If who you are, is in line with your chosen career and your level of success, the fire can continually burn hotter. As you grow, you will find yourself naturally adding coals to the fire. However, if your success begins to blow harder, and your fire burns hotter without your finding more coals, because you have neglected your inner growth, or because you have no natural interest and talent in what you are doing, you will find the heat of the furnace beginning to consume, instead of enthuse you."

They spoke on this topic for some time, Selsan always driving the Messenger back to thinking from the inside, outwards – always focusing first on who people were, then on their achievements. He showed him how, almost invariably, those who had achieved great things from weak characters, eventually found their lives crumbling around them.

A Death brings Opportunity

The THREE FUNDAMENTAL ATTITUDES of the HEART of the LEADER:
   - **a deep seated genuine concern for the well-being of his people**
   - **a deep belief in every person's ability and desire to improve self and environment**
   - **a firm belief in his own ability to be instrumental in this process of improvement**

Things in the Great Castle of Suran suddenly underwent a great change. Cresan, the trusted High Councillor and chief recorder of Leondar, died in old age. King Suran was no fool, and although he really cared for his people he had long ago recognized in himself an inability, apparently inherited from his father, to really command loyalty. He knew Selsan's loyalty to him was born out of the depth of Selsan's character, and his ability to see beyond the King's weaknesses a true desire to do what was best for his country.

However, his own insecurities had always prevented him from appointing anyone with Selsan's strength of character to his own court.

While he was grieving over the death of Cresan, who was almost like a father to him, King Suran was thinking about all the people in his court. He had no son. He knew there were already some rivalling and fighting and that more than one young man already had plans for how they would take over the kingdom, upon the king's death.

He was not a young man any more. Sometimes he looked at the young men in his court and saw in their eyes the expressions of vultures, waiting for him to die. None of them really cared for Leondar, or for the people. He knew he wasn't the best of leaders. An inherent laziness had prevented him from applying himself to study, despite Cresan's nagging, so his skills never really improved. He compensated for these by hiding behind the High Council and a strong Royal Guard. From the outside he looked strong and majestic. The Great King Suran. But he knew that Cresan had seen through it all. He also believed that Selsan saw through it all.

~~~

Suran suffered from a common leadership problem:
His public image was not congruent with his true character.
The outside of his life was much bigger than the inside, so that his life
was like a balloon threatening to pop at any moment.

~~~

42

Whilst thinking about all this, there was a gentle knock from the door behind him. Only Selsan and Cresan ever dared to knock at his door. Everyone else always waited for him to appear.

"Come in, Selsan!" The King was secretly relieved. He didn't turn around. Maybe Selsan could give him some advice.

"I apologize for disturbing Your Highness." The voice was young. The Great King Suran swung around, for a moment furious that anyone would disturb him. However, he saw no fear on the face of his young Royal Chief Messenger – who was also not all that young any more. There was too much grief and tiredness etched in the lines of the face, to allow room for fear.

"I have ridden from Selsan's court on the communications horses. He asked I must convey my condolences and his pledge of support of any kind needed, the moment I set foot in the castle. I also want to convey to you the same, from myself, Your Highness. Selsan could not come, himself, immediately, for as you are aware, the changes of last year still place continuous pressure on his schedule."

Suran's anger was immediately abated. He realized it were two days from the Great Castle of Leondar to Selsan's castle, using the communications horses. These horses were always kept ready, two hours ride apart, to deliver any urgent messages to and from any one of the three castles in Leondar. It has been only three days and one night, since Cresan's death.

"You must have ridden, at full gallop, with no rest for two days and a night!"

"Yes, Your Majesty. I felt this was a time in which you needed any real support you could get."

The Great King Suran could see the genuineness in the eyes, the true concern, but even deeper, in the words, he read true understanding. He realized that, probably through his spending as much time as he could justify, in Selsan's court, this young man had gained wisdom that penetrates outer appearances. This man understood the true impact Cresan's death could have on the kingdom.

"I want you to go and get a good night's rest. Refresh yourself. Ask the royal kitchen to prepare any food you desire. Strengthen your heart. Tomorrow we will speak. I will need you to be strong, and I will need that weary look and the grief on your face to be gone."

The Messenger obeyed, feeling there was nothing more he could do for the king right now. After a good meal, he fell down on one of the soft palace beds and almost immediately sleep folded its blanket of comfort over him.

The next morning, as the first rays of the sun broke over the eastern horizon of Leondar, the rays touching the tips of the Great Castle of Leondar found the Messenger looking out over the land. His heart was troubled. His grief for Cresan was great, because Cresan had also been like a father to him, but his concern for Leondar was greater. Cresan had always guided the king's decisions, and Cresan had the wisdom and insight to understand the true future impact of changes.

The king really cared for his land. The Messenger had no doubt of this. He was also wise, and he understood many things. However, he lacked the depth of character to face crises with a calm countenance. He lacked the strength to discipline and control his people, and he lacked the knowledge to make his wisdom truly useful.

The Messenger recalled a conversation he had had with Cresan once:

"Why does the king not simply get rid of Nashin?" the Messenger wanted to know. Both he and Cresan could clearly see Nashin was failing.

"You have to understand something about the former King Rennan, to understand this. King Rennan, unlike Suran, didn't care for his people in the least. However, like Suran, he had a weakness in his own confidence and inner strength. So he resorted to a continuous display of his outer strength to compensate for this. You had observed to me previously that King Suran hides behind his guard and his great palace and the High Councillors. So his father hid mostly behind an ability to execute judgement swiftly, without asking questions.

"King Suran is so afraid of becoming a tyrant like his father that he doesn't want to discipline anyone. However, at the same time, he has never learnt to confidently tell someone that they are doing a bad job, and to help them and give them opportunity to change. He can see the people suffering under Nashin, but he doesn't have the strength to deal with Nashin."

~~~

Misplaced humility can do as much harm as pride

~~~

As the Messenger was thinking about this, he started thinking about all the untamed and uncontrolled ambition he had seen in the palace. He realized that as much as he had respected Cresan, even Cresan had failed the kingdom, because he didn't become a buffer to compensate for his leader's weaknesses. Cresan had the strength of character and the wisdom – he could have helped by guiding the hearts and the thoughts of the young people – but he didn't. He always felt that it "wasn't his place".

He was too humble, the Messenger thought.

From the roof of the Great Castle, the Messenger was able to see miles and miles of the Great Southern planes stretched out before him. He could see the Big River dividing the East and the West, curling like a dragon, seeming to protect some of its children on the one side, and ignore the suffering of the ones on the other. One could, even from this distance, see the chaos that was busy setting into the West. In the East, he could see the clear lines of the farms. He could see a good distribution of green and yellow and brown – meaning that some fields were ready for harvest, some would be ready in the future, and others were ready for the next planting.

In the West, the lines between the farms had become distorted. The battles for borderlines were never ending. Nashin had a full time peace-keeping force trying to keep this problem at bay.

What would happen to the kingdom, if the people started seeing through King Suran's façade? What would happen if one of these ambitious young men gained a big enough following to overthrow the King? Would the Royal Guard follow a new king or would they protect Suran? Would they go to war against Selsan, if Selsan resisted the change?

Absorbed in his thoughts, he didn't notice that the King had been walking towards him. He started when he suddenly heard the footsteps behind him.

"Your Majesty." The Messenger bowed.

"I didn't expect you to be up this early. What are you thinking of?"

"I was just looking at the land, your Majesty," the Messenger was trying to think what to say. He felt this was a good opportunity to suggest some action, but he wasn't sure what action and he didn't want to offend the king, "and I know Cresan had made much effort to try and assist with the conditions in the West. You will recall that, after the transition, he took responsibility as recorder and High Councillor for the West, by his own choice." The Messenger didn't know how to continue, but King Suran noticed his discomfort, and ventured a suggested completion of his thoughts.

"And with your wisdom, you could not have missed the fact that any good done in the West, had really been Cresan's, and not Nashin's doing. So you are afraid that, with Cresan gone, the West will now very rapidly fall into total chaos."

The messenger didn't answer. He just nodded his head, and sadly looked over the land before them.

"I want to ask you to become my Second in Command."

There was no introduction, none of the king's normal well-polished oration – a simple request from one man to another. The Messenger was totally taken aback.

"That is a tremendous honour for a man of my age, Your Majesty!"

"Yes. As you know, I have no son. There are few of the young men in the court I can trust, and none of those I do trust have much wisdom. The reason they can be trusted is because they are too simple to be ambitious. I believe, however that you truly carry the interests of Leondar in your heart. I have watched you these years, and with purpose I have assigned you to Selsan that you may learn. This was part of Cresan's advice to me also. A decree will be written, that upon my sudden death, you will receive the crown. However, as I grow older, I will at some stage hand the reigns over to you, so I can retire in peace."

The Messenger was at a loss for words.

"I apologize for my silence, your Majesty. I do not know what to say."

"Are you, then not prepared to grant me this request?"

"Of course I am, your Majesty. I am very grateful, indeed, for the privilege, and the opportunity. However, I doubt my own ability for this task."

That same afternoon, the ceremony was performed. Under different circumstances, this would have been the greatest day of the Messenger's life, but he was still grieved for Cresan, and during the ceremony he could almost taste the jealousy in the air, as he looked over some of the king's officials.

More than ever before, did he realize that the king had surrounded himself with men of personal ambition. Their ambition probably looked good – made them look like they were the kind of people that could get things done – but the king seemed to fail to realize that personal ambition and true concern for the land and its people were two character traits that found living together in the same home, very difficult.

The Messenger dispatched two delegations to invite Selsan and Nashin to the Great Castle. In the few days, awaiting their arrival, he had meetings with all the High Officials. He used the meetings not only to begin to understand the condition of all the various aspects of the kingdom, but also to try and gauge their characters.

He was deeply disappointed. Although many of the officials were well skilled, they lacked character. None of them seemed to care for the people or for Leondar. Some of them seemed to have some passion for the projects they were running, but mostly it seemed like they were more concerned now with impressing him, than what they were with really doing a good job. Many of them had developed their skills of oration far beyond their skills of government. Almost all of them seemed to lack the ability to think deeply and understand the long term impact of what they were doing.

Many of them were executing projects initiated by Cresan or by King Suran himself, without understanding the true purpose of the projects –

and so they often went adrift in their activities – side-tracked by their own agendas or simply by lack of understanding of where they needed to be going.

He also found them to be competitive and reluctant to share problems and successes with one another. Having spent so much time in Selsan's court, he had become used to the fact that leaders at a high level shared the responsibility for the welfare of the land, and consequently were always ready to bring their problems to the table to find the quickest solutions amongst the meeting of minds. Here, he realized that the minds were spending their energy in thinking of ways to prove themselves one greater than another.

Eventually he decided that, in lieu of the lack of appropriate people being available to fulfil the current void, he would just work harder, and take the responsibilities on himself. He knew that not much remained to do in order to be the High Councillor to the East, so he would begin to take over Cresan's responsibilities in the West, and he was sure that he would still have time available, to attend to more general matters in the kingdom.

A few days later, Selsan's carriage rolled into the Great Courtyard, and he was received by the Messenger and King Suran, with great joy. He immediately expressed his condolences before they retired to one of the roof gardens.

Selsan glowed with pride when he heard that the Messenger had been appointed as King Suran's right hand. He could hardly express his congratulations in words.

"So now I must call you Your Highness!" Selsan laughed as they sat down in a garden that overlooked the Southern Planes.

"Yes, and you must bow." The Messenger jested, but he was also bursting with the honest pride he felt to be allowed to be in this position, and that Selsan, who had done so much for him, would be so generous in his congratulations. He regarded Selsan as his personal mentor, and he felt there was no greater way in which he would ever have been able to reward Selsan's mentorship than to have achieved this. He knew that without Selsan, he would probably today still just be a messenger.

After they had spoken for a short while King Suran asked to be excused.

The Messenger immediately began sharing his concern regarding the King's court, with Selsan.

"I cannot even find one person I would be confident to promote and assign to you as High Councillor, and even less so, one that would be able to deal with Nashin."

Selsan listened attentively, interrupting with a few questions here and there.

"Firstly," he began once the messenger had finished, "you must relinquish this idea of doing all the work yourself. By doing that, you are already admitting your inability to lead in a difficult environment – you are choosing the easy way – working harder – rather than the difficult way – developing people and giving them opportunities. You have to lead, and if you now swamp yourself with an endless task list of activities, you will find yourself unable to have the time, the energy or the freedom of mind, to think deeply about solving problems.

~~~

Insecurity will tempt a leader to do the work that his people should be doing

~~~

One of the things you must remember is that most people are ambitious. If you were going to try and build a court of people like yourself, you would probably have to travel the whole world, and still you would hardly find half the people you need.

However, ambition can be a resource to you. Remember how I always taught you to match people to resources. And remember how I taught you that sometimes, you have no people for the resource. What do you have to do then?"

"Train – create skill; and speak – create interest and passion." The Messenger recalled.

"That's right. Now you have never learnt how to use the resource of ambition. It is a powerful resource, and you will find it everywhere where you rise up in leadership. Few people rise in leadership like you, on pure concern for others. Most rise out of partial concern for themselves, and partial concern for others. Some are only concerned for themselves, but pure self-concern is not as common as many think.

Now, when planning to use a new resource, what were the first things you needed to know?"

"What kind of people and what kind of skills were needed, to develop the resource – and for that, I needed to understand something about the resource."

"Yes." Selsan kept quiet for a while, and the Messenger knew this was his queue. Selsan wasn't going to say more.

The Messenger sat for some time, in deep thought. If Selsan's comments were true, then he realized that, wherever he would want to be a leader, he would come across personal ambition. That meant that in order to be a good leader, he would have to learn how to use ambition as his resource, rather than his enemy. Up to now, he had only seen the negative effects of ambition, but according to Selsan, there was a positive side to this.

He suddenly realized that ambition is really simply about the desire to be successful, for one's own sake. It was just like his wanting to be successful for the people's sake. Therefore, the desire was the same – it was just the object that differed. The desire was for success.

~~~

All people want to be successful.
What the leader defines as success will shape his people's hearts

~~~

What was success in Selsan's court? It was the benefit of all the people. Over years, Selsan had taught his leaders to see that as success.

What was success in King Suran's court? Position. You could speak to anyone, and ask them who was the most successful in the court, and they would tell you that he, the Messenger, had just proven to be most successful – and the servants were the least successful. So they had become to believe in position as their criteria for success. But position becomes more and more limited the higher you go. There can be only one king, and one right hand to the king, two regional governors and four, or sometimes, at most, five High Councillors.

With the Messenger having grasped this truth, they continued to discuss a plan to begin to systematically change the perceptions of success in the king's court. During this discussion, Selsan taught the Messenger the principle of leading through serving.

"Instead of designing a plan," he was explaining, "and then delegating the tasks, you first transfer the vision and the purpose of the vision. Once you've transferred the vision, you let them work out the plan, and you become available as an advisor and an assistant. They get the right to request of you to do things they cannot, such as approving special funds, dispatching royal equipment or discussing certain issues with the king. They take ownership of their projects, and you assist them. You no longer give orders; you receive and execute requests from them. But be very careful to not accept requests to do anything they could have done for themselves.

~~~

It doesn't matter if the cat is black or white, what matters is if the cat can catch the mouse

~~~

"When doing this, you will find that they will begin to do things differently to the way you would have done it. You must be careful to communicate the core purpose of what you are trying to achieve, and learn to put aside your personal preferences regarding how it should be done. If you had ox-wagons in mind and they want to use donkey carts, put your preference aside unless there is a substantial reason for it. Remember always the purpose of what you are trying to achieve, which is to develop their leadership.

Keeping people focused on the purpose of their activities, greatly enhances their personal sense of fulfilment and self-actualization

"This takes a load off your shoulders, but more importantly, it feeds their desire for self-actualization. They begin to feel that they make the decisions, and when a project achieves its goals, they begin to sense success. Position awareness becomes vaguer, because there is no longer a command-and-obey relationship, but a request-and-assist relationship between people of different levels.

"Make sure they keep focused on the vision and the purpose you initially placed before them. This is especially important in the beginning, because they do not yet know your heart. The longer you've worked together, the more you will find them catching on to your ideas, and keeping on track, because they understand and share your heart."

Realizing that the biggest change first had to happen in the way he was leading, the Messenger thought through all his officials again, and decided on four officials he would nominate as the High Councillors responsible for representing the two regions in the king's court.

To change the way things are, change the way you lead

The next day Nashin also arrived, and the meetings were called. The four officials were brought in one by one, and put through gruelling interviews. Having changed the way he perceived ambition, the Messenger now found that he felt less threatened by their jealousy, and found that their ambition no longer seemed to cast a shadow over all their good qualities. By the end of two days, he felt that any one of the four could possibly do a good job.

The two new High Councillors were appointed, the appointment ceremony was held, and things returned to their normal routines.

The Beginnings of Improvement

INFLUENCE is real leadership
He who sways the hearts of the people, is the real leader

Although the Messenger really wanted to improve conditions for the people of the West of Leondar, he realized that it was still not within his power to make all the changes he knew was needed.

However, he began to immediately change the way in which King Suran's court was managed, and tried to get everyone to better understand the purpose of the king's court. Having dealt with his prejudice against ambition, the people seemed less jealous now, and over time he perceived that most of them began to really respect his leadership, as he respected each one of them.

He spoke about "genuine concern for the people" until he felt the words were ringing in his ears at night – but over time, he began to notice more and more of his leaders beginning to notice the needs of the people in the West. Over time without his giving any instructions to that effect, he noticed a gradual increase in the projects that were proposed and initiated, for improvements in the West.

Realizing that he was not able to get rid of Nashin without compromising Suran, he began to make a very special effort to put his personal dislikes of him aside, and began to make every attempt to build a relationship of trust and confidence between the two of them. Although their value systems were vastly different, the Messenger was certain that he would be able to find in himself the depth of character to work around Nashin's flaws, and help him improve his region. For the sake of the people, he knew this had to be done.

The Messenger succeeded in building a very strong relationship of trust between himself and the High Councillor responsible for Nashin's region. This High Councillor, in his turn, seemed to be of a character more or less half way between that of the Messenger and Nashin, and this High Councillor soon had built a relationship of similar trust between himself and Nashin. Although the East still continued to outperform the West in every aspect, the West did improve, under the subtle guidance of the Messenger and his trusted High Councillor; and without Nashin's noticing, they planted many ideas of improvement in his mind, and helped with the implementation of those.

They also began to look at some of the good things that were happening in the East and where possible, began to enforce the performing of certain duties by law – which compelled Nashin to create more order in his region.

If all else fails, use rules

The Messenger still regularly visited Selsan, but for shorter periods of time. He always took pains to have carefully thought about every one of his greatest problems, and had the best questions he could think of prepared for Selsan.

He always returned either with solutions which Selsan, with careful questioning had guided him into discovering for himself, or with a set of questions he had to consider for some time, and find the answers to.

The real leader is the person with the real influence

The Great King Suran's kingdom grew in wealth and power, as time continued. King Suran soon perceived that, although his crown and his staff and his ring were the symbols of the highest leadership of the country, the real leader was the Messenger. However, he was content, because he saw improvement, and the Messenger, for the sake of the stability of the kingdom, continued to make the Great King Suran great in the eyes of the people.

The Messenger, though perceiving that his activities provided the true leadership in the kingdom, was always humbled by the knowledge that these were based on what he had learnt over many years, mostly under the guidance of Selsan.

Epilogue

The footpath in the forest against the foggy slopes of the most Northern Mountains of Leondar was overgrown from disuse. The horse was breathing hard, steam coming out of its nostrils as its warm breath clashed with the icy mountain air. The rider was dressed in the clothes of a regular man of the mountains, a hood covering his features.

It took about three hours of negotiating the steep and winding little path, before the small plateau with the little clearance was reached. Smoke was coming out of the chimney of the solitary little hut, and the windows were glowing a warm yellow colour in the rapidly descending darkness.

The traveller settled his horse in the stable, before knocking on the rough door. An old man opened, and smiled when he recognized the traveller.

Inside, the hut was simple but spacious. It consisted only of a large single room. The one side of the room had a fireplace with some cooking utensils, two beds, two writing desks with some writing equipment, and two comfortable chairs. The rest of the room was filled with shelves and shelves full of old books and scrolls, from roof to floor.

After a hearty dinner, they sat down to long deep discussions. The traveller spoke first, only to be interrupted here and there, by questions from the old man.

The old man was making little notes on a piece of paper at his desk. Sometimes he would stop the traveller, and write for a while, before letting him continue.

When the traveller finally had finished, the old man began to ask him questions. The questions were deep and difficult questions – because they related to the deep and difficult problems the traveller had shared. They were questions that required a deep understanding of one's own character, one's own strengths and weaknesses, as well as those of other people. They required a good understanding of matters of the heart as well as the mind. They required an understanding of what made people do what they do. They required much knowledge and deep insight into this knowledge.

The traveller knew that there was not a single right answer to any of the questions, but he had learnt long ago, that there were wrong answers. He knew that a right answer constituted that it would solve the problem, and benefit the people, but some questions had right answers, good answers and better answers. The answers to some questions depended very much on who was asking the question.

Some questions he had no answers to. At these, the old man made some more notes.

Afterwards, they slept, and the next morning, they old man gave the traveller a piece of paper with some unresolved questions on it. The traveller began to work through the questions to which he had had no answers the night before. The old man helped him to think through these and rephrase until he had found the right questions, because that was always a good start for finding good answers. He used the scrolls and the books for references. These were collections of works from all over the world written by great kings and scholars, some many years dead, some alive still.

Every time he believed he had arrived at an answer, they had long discussions about the answer, before he would continue to the next question. There were one or two questions to which they could find no answers.

This continued for several days.

Finally, the traveller was ready to leave again.

It was early morning, and the sun had just risen over the ridge of the Eastern Mountains. The traveller and the old man hugged. The traveller donned his cloak, hooded his face again and mounted his horse.

"See you just before the winter, King Rennan." He greeted.

"I will try to think of some answers to those outstanding questions," The old man replied, "but remember Selsan, above all, love your people!"

About the Author

It has taken me a long time to figure out what I really am interested and passionate about. After school I did some mission work, then did compulsory service in the defence force for two years, and thereafter found a job as an office cleaner in a cardboard factory. From there I went into the insurance industry where I was reasonably successful and desperately unhappy.

Quitting in sheer desperation, I tried to start a business, failed miserably, and after several months of living on bread and potatoes, went back into insurance. I got a good pay-back from tax because of the period that I was without income, and used that to pay for the studies an exams to become a Microsoft Certified Systems Engineer. For a few years I was very happy working in the IT industry, became manager, and later national operations manager. I worked 7 days a week, 16 hours a day, leading the department to pretty astounding results, while also leading a youth group on the side for one of the largest churches in our city – and then promptly burnt out.

I took a break, went to China, wrote this book, went back to "normal" work, began to do some management consulting and became strategic manager and later director of a non-profit organisation. From here I started lecturing at a university, and found some opportunities consulting more in the international market – which brought me to where I am today, as change management coordinator for the China plant of an international off-shore company.

During all this time, I continually studied, and completed first a Bachelors in Management and then a Masters in Managing and Leading Innovation and Change.

I am fascinated by, and therefore incessantly read and write about the integration of design, purpose and calling with performance and success as a foundation for living a successful, fulfilling and meaningful life; and about the way this scales into the design, purpose, performance and success of teams, organisations, and societies.

Ashton Fourie
22 May 2015
Xiamen, China
ashton@ashtonfourie.com

www.ingramcontent.com/pod-product-compliance
Lightning Source LLC
Chambersburg PA
CBHW072310200526
45168CB00014B/1190